Two Doors

Julia Gibson

Poems by Julia Gibson
Clare Songbirds Publishing House Poetry Series
ISBN 978-1-947653-76-4
Clare Songbirds Publishing House
Two Doors© 2019 Julia Gibson

All Rights Reserved. Clare Songbirds Publishing House retains right to reprint.
Permission to reprint individual poems must be obtained from the author who owns the copyright.

Printed in the United States of America
FIRST EDITION

Clare Songbirds Publishing House Mission Statement:
Clare Songbirds Publishing House was established to provide a print forum for the creation of limited edition, fine art from poets and writers, both established and emerging. We strive to reignite and continue a tradition of quality, accessible literary arts to the national and international community of writers, and readers. Chapbook manuscripts are carefully chosen for their ability to propel the expansion of art and ideas in literary form. We provide an accessible way to promote the art of words in order to resonate with, and impact, readers not yet familiar with the siren song of poets and writers. Clare Songbirds Publishing House espouses a singular cultural development where poetry creates community and becomes commonplace in public places.

140 Cottage Street
Auburn, New York 13021
www.claresongbirdspub.com

Contents

Prologue   6

Part I
My Kingdom Thee   8
Ballade   9
Where We Return To   10
Presence   11
Billowing Out   12
Water Like Thought   13
Humming   14
A Hand of Each Weight   15
Upon Turning Over   16
For No Lack of Better Words   17
On Scrap Paper   18
Before He Wakes   19
Mischief   20
Trust   21
Courting April   22
Nowhere Else To Be   23
You Gave Me New Shape   24
Air and Flame   25
Turning Toward   26
The Electric Breakfast Slide   27
Partner   28
Talking   29
After Much Bedroom Idleness   30

Part II
Medium   32
What Comes Next   33
The Leap   34
Widening of the Ways   35
Watcher   36
Marriage For All   37
Water Acro   38
Picnic Blanket   39
A Moment Bottled For You   40
Vision of Another Self   41
Ergo, Ego, Go   42
Daydream of You, Who Are Far Away   43
Just Kids   44
Connection   45
Embers   46

Blowing on Coals	47
Wealth	48
Assurance	49
Contact	50
Crows	51
Caution to the Winds	52

Part III

Rolling Away the Stone	54
One Breath of Flame	55
Poison From the Wound	56
Forest Fire	57
Page Not Found	58
Siphon	59
The Verdant Doorway	60
Following the Trail	61
One Promise	62
Honing	63
A Tower of the Mind	64
Traded Time	65
To Hatred Transmute	66
Bothered	67
The Tiger and the Turtle	68
Flitting, Steadfast	7
Ripe	70
Rhyme	71
Favorite	72
The Hard Way	73
Determined	74
Cumulus	75
Exchange	76
Crutches	77
Kingdom Come	78
Epilogue	79

This is for you.
What will you do with it?

Prologue

Do you trust me?
That is the question.
Do you trust me enough
to take my words into yourself
to echo in your thoughts
or even the body of your emotions?

Some poets speak
with both such authority
and compassion
that it doesn't matter
whether they are right.
It is the light behind the words
that you believe.

Part I

My Kingdom Thee

If I were not to love the stars you speak,
would I not mute mine ears with cursèd leaf
so plucked from boughs God laid before the meek
and beg of virtue's host temptation brief?
If summer's eve sang not a note so pure,
and dreaming dimmed beyond horizon's curve,
would I not falter still at winter's door
or seal away the life that I deserve?
But garden's groves untamed my feet doth tread,
toward moons that wax along the river's tides
and grace the skies which honeyed clouds embed,
to echo sounds my solemn heart confides.
If love's fulfillment wicked trespass be,
then heaven not worth grasping, my kingdom thee.

Ballade

I wish that there were more love songs for men.
Just as women could revel in the power to move,
so men could revel in the spell of being wooed.

You are who I want, the song implies, boldly
do I seek you out
and better myself on your behalf:

> As unexpected rain pours from some Deva realm
> like a sprinkling of meteorites all over my
> skin, I purify my heart for you with discipline.

For your gentleness and warmth earn admiration;
your beauty beckons delighting in all its days;
your zeal for life deserves complete partner.

Here I am, the song crescendos,
here I will be in bed each morning
luminous so as to see you,
curious so as to know you
and discover hidden star worlds
to bring back to you.

You can let go, rest undefended
in your body and your spirit;
I will protect and watch over you,
be the keeper of your stories,
be a witness to your experience
as it continually blooms.

Where We Return To

It took six hours to retrace the strokes
that it took three months to make.
The plane went up like a whale
arched and diving down into its midnight sky,
and the whole of Los Angeles twinkled,
embedded in the earth, like a volcanic stone
cut in a million different places.
Somewhere, making a parallel jet stream
my bike was cinched in the belly of another whale
glutted with piles of krill in the cargo hold.

The long, sprawling stream
of roads, desert, mountain passes
wound up into a maelstrom spanning sea to sea
to carry me up from their mire
marked by milestones of letters and quiet wishes
to the spot where I imagined
meeting you again.

I had watched the Pacific condense
out of the mists before me
into an impenetrable mirror of moonbeams,
and I could almost feel your warmth
seeping through your shirt
as I paused behind you on the pier
at Narragansett Bay
as you, leaning on the railing, gazed
as though at the glints of surfacing whales
on the path of their migration.

Presence

Heat billows in blooms around my neck,
clouds of it spilling over into September.

When I remember the shiver-shock of your fingers
searing into and blowing up my consciousness,

I become fervent in my embrace of feeling
all the transient touches of life.

This fan blows tendrils of half-damp hair
across my forehead, to the floor

where my palms and every finger press down
then lift, interrupt the golden ceiling light.

And the joy I could have if I were dancing
every second of my life becomes real

for a handful of vital beats, when my body
listens intently to the small voices of the world:

highway blur, synthetic shimmers, the raps
of a hammer on a desk with some assembly required.

Billowing Out

In a time glazed with cricket song,
lying on the glossy, sunshiny grass,
your pulse makes little thrums in your wrist,
like the rustling of a sail.
And oh yes, would I like to float away with you,
you and your dark luster, warm touch, soft eyes
that know my body, and in shadows along my back
take delight.
That some things become clear
outside the one-way tunnel of time —
inherited by ease of convention —
is a hunch I feel, so aware
as I am in this peace, which can be made
eternal in all directions.

Water Like Thought

Thrown by the bathroom window,
the moon skips across dark water like a stone,
flicked into the fog of 2am memory.

I stumble back toward sleep and vow to recall
exactly how it was, when the morning blinks.
I hold up my hand to the greyed-out wall
to meld its shadow with the projections of trees.

This is one of the few bottles with a message
that floated back to me —
a rare skipped stone that boomeranged
across dark water into my seeking hand.

Humming

Your face, eclipsing sunset glare,
just cresting the wind-swept hill, hair burnished
over squinting eyes and shimmering cheekbones;
and the sidewalk still, particles sparkling.
Some moments feel like crystals in the hand,
like electric drumbeat chants,
like fizzing touches and brushes with "sin".
And in this landscape set ablaze
fingers mingle, sounding ripples through the air.

A Hand of Each Weight

A sopping bird's nest dangling over soaking bark
within the warm, percolating hiss of rain —
everything in its present place, but you cannot choose
that which stays and that which fades away.

Graffiti murals rippling on the fieldstone wall,
graffiti blazed in black on street lamp poles,
graffiti scratched upon a crumpled page —
through blundering incompetence or timely change,
it will all fade away. But rooted in this present place,
so too might foolishness burn away, leaving
grace.

Upon Turning Over

The window pane becomes a stage
for the spotlight of the fresh sun.
Beaming through the motes of dust,
the rising remnants of life's rust,
its sparks alight gently upon his lashes.

Whisper thin and fanning soft
against my floating lips,
they rustle with his sleeping breaths
that I cherish, seeping tears.

For No Lack of Better Words

Why must I be *falling* in love?
If it pleases me,
why may I not leap?
Why may I not exult in it,
or dance or bask or swim in it
in the common tongue?

For I know that I am singing in it,
I am walking it out to Stevie Wonder,
with jauntiness and spring of hip.
And god knows that I am
overflowing with it,
that my body cannot contain
and so radiates it,
and that when my energies are spent
so gloriously, to give off rays of it,
I lay glistening in my bed and
find my sanctuary and my peace in it.

On Scrap Paper

One
word
I
want
to
say:

I
am
bursting
at
the
lips

with
love
I
cannot
give
its
voice.

So
here
is
a
little
fragment
to
keep
in
your
pocket

like
a
piece
of
good
luck.

Before He Wakes

One of my favorite things in life
is when the light strikes in
askance, upon bare skin, which then
plummets into soft relief where shadows bend
along shoulder curves which wend
down the spinal valley floor.
They emerge again, down the dipping corridor
that ends in the dusting by the sun,
its mist of diamonds upon eyelashes and fingertips.

How could such a silence not be resplendent
with other glories ripe for the seeing
for the first time
and for savoring in new depths?
How could such a silence not make one breathe
in a more tenacious and loving embrace
of existing in human form upon this earth
for whatever eternity and quiver of a wing is ours?

Mischief

I am looking for an angle
in the wild amber sea
to watch my bird-man tumble,
like a puma in the leaves.

You know my eyes in darkness
glinting keenly in the night;
you know I circle out there
to pounce on you mid-flight.

I am looking from an angle,
slipped between the trees.
You think you see a shadow;
I am a beast of subtle breed.

In the smoky edge of dusk
you're caught in pooling sun;
you glance over your shoulder
and know the game's begun.

Once, in waves of strangers,
you spy me from afar,
but I am gone before you blink again
in the flickering fog of stars.

You think you are safe from being prey,
then from above you hear:
"Look out, my little bird-man,
your dance with me is near."

My dominion is the wild,
and you are no match for me;
you're trapped within my golden snare
—you will surrender to be free.

Trust

We are calf-deep in cerulean, gold-tipped,
with waning sunshine leaning long
into the woods which ripen
from green to grape.
One of these nights, when I discover
that yours is a heart I can lean into,
I will tell you of the slammed door, slammed
the same way every time —
whose shudders through the walls
I can still feel within me.
I will tell you that I blamed myself
and I told myself, many nights, maybe
she will love me again tomorrow —
so that I would not also cry alone.

It is not so that you will be sad for me;
we are, each one of us,
both blighted and blessed.
It is so that when I show you my fear
of betraying what I could be
you will understand.

And I show you so that,
as we run underneath the blind leaves
in the twinkling hours of night
with you, maybe
I can let it go.

Courting April

A renegade star balloon is waywardly escaped,
looping willy-nilly above a 'Missing Unicorn' sign
on a yellowy mellow Sunday afternoon.
Change billows in continuous,
and against the ocean it springs upon the land
in bewildering flirtations of purple,
and peach, and lightly poking greens.
"Not just yet," rustle the daffodils,
"Come again tomorrow," whistle the elms.
But tease for tease I am a ready match,
groomed in patience by a gauntlet of frost-laden walks,
and tomorrow I shall come back, you can be sure,
to steal a noontime kiss.

Nowhere Else To Be

Night clouds glide through the atmosphere
behind the black fingers of the maple tree.
Briefly, stars are laid naked by their passage,
then made secret again by the gray-mauve gauze.
The fingers twirl smoke tendrils between them
like ribbons that tango in order
to part in dissolution.
I drum fingers upon the wood
and riff upon the jazz
whose swoops blend into the vernal wind.
Three friends around a table pass the pipe
from island to island, hand to hand.

Speckled with floodlight, sodden leaves and drooping grass;
shadows strung up along the fence, and they form
a clothesline of fluttering projections
that I behold through the washed-out technicolor swirl
shining through my eyelashes from the street lamp.
Between two lungs, a heart like the coal
smoldering and spritzing light,
a puck-shaped sparkler, *la coeur*
reverberating with rumors of crocuses.

You Gave Me New Shape

Bobbing grapes, like buoys,
and faraway sailboats
skim slowly across the two lakes,
both poisoned, clear and deep;
golden ripples
swing hypnotically toward sleep.

One wants a place to feel oneself
a point against the swirling swaths
of blue and white,
where vertigree froths in season,
past the brim
of jutting promontories
that the patient water trims.

You made me a vessel, and I refill myself
to hold up to your lips of dusky crimson,
a pearlen bowl of nectar, with every-color light
dusting chin and arcing eyelash kites.

Air and Flame

The breath, it makes a mooring post
when wading into mist.
Its count sounds surely in my mind
when the next step disappears.
I have studied its eddies and its tides,
and the time has come to abandon charts
and navigate by the stars.

Unburdened by heavy foliations of the past,
bound in brittle, static reams,
I listen all around, can move nimbly again.
Breaths that were shallow and compressed
now round out in full.

And from afar there is just the stray rustling
of a few summer-lapping leaves
that breathe in a thousand places,
whose internal weather
knows no captain,
with barely a vane to swing
or witness to record.

Turning Toward

Sometimes I watch what seem
like ordinary flutters of existence,
such as when you swallow, or breathe.
And I have, in a quiet pause, counted your eyelashes,
convex and contrasting against the wall,
and traced the sheen of your eyelids
from soft corner to soft corner.
I am entranced by these moments
of your bewildering, complex being.

But my wonder and my loves,
my principles and my promises,
are in their degrees untested.
We needn't affect a dramatic pose
and contemplate choice as a skull in the hand
held away from the body,
wearing the anguish of a fallen angel
upon our brow. After all, each present time
we think we hold, already lost as soon
as we know it is happening.
All that is needed is
when it is time to step through to another
passageway of who we can be,
we close the door behind us softly
and let go the handle.

The Electric Breakfast Slide

I am the pajama poet
grooving on invisible keys in blanket and socks
with the ripe, jazzy blasts of Funk
rolling through the greasy-scented kitchen.
Why not answer the day with a dance party?

The snow's not melting fast enough,
the dishes don't get cleaned enough,
can't figure what to do in life enough,
so why not dance?

swing it, swing it, swing it, bop,
workit, workit, workit, pop
Let me hold you tight now baby,
you know just how to sway me baby,

you know what to do.

Partner

Is it your heart or mine
that sends quivers through our cores
then through our shirts,
pressed and bunched up in between
our parting embrace?

I am almost a clean and empty shell
through which the wind can whistle
but for a thimble-full of ocean,
pooled and lingering in deep curvature.

This may be the last time I feel your warmth,
but so was yesterday —
and the next one-millionth of a second.
Do I grieve for every increment of absence?

We live just one infinitesimal at a time
at whatever speed we choose.
There are always things to look forward to
independent of things;
my joy is largely of my own making.

But still,
you are my secret tenderness
and steward of my vulnerability.
You are not everything,
but you help me grow my happiness
and that within me which is good.

Talking

I felt a ripple in my veins
as the spring wind made rustle through the grass
and the shirtsleeves on our shoulders brushed —
shivering, but aching not to move
lest the moment slip beyond the sky.

Our voices wove a silver braid
holding me fast to the hammock slats,
and the baying of a dog
anchored our buoyant space —
for the intimate expanse seemed
always about to rise
with my glances at the points
of shining in your eyes.

Yesterday the frosted mesh of trees
floated noiselessly above our steps,
and the slick bricks of the sidewalk crept
beneath us toward that playground gate;
and so I remembered that first ripple in my veins.

After Much Bedroom Idleness

One full turn passes, the blinds crack apart
and then divide the first peach streams,
all the way through to moonlight.
Earlier along this blessed arc,
you had no idea how gracefully your foot outstretched
illumined and pale like a sublime sketch
in the pages of the book on Leonardo
that spreads its glossy wings upon the chair.

How much of ourselves do we never perceive
through our blindspotted spyglass?
But even distorted of sight and scarce aware,
a humble and sometimes happy fate,
still I feel a vision, clear
and closing upon the heart of things,
of the wonder and teetering beauty of this world.
It is always straining to break though
and ever just bursting out
from behind grey and damming window blinds.

Part II

Medium

In the ocean a single bit of foam,
in a single bit of foam, an ocean.
The bubbles of the milky froth
burgeon and burst like city lights
seen from afar, swirling and spinning
about the dark center of the glass
like a scattering of pinprick stars.

The cool clash of steam and draft
flickers over cheeks and eyelids;
hands begin to flush with heat
whose singe begins to surge.

To hold on, or to let go?
In a microcosmic moment of flesh to stone
I witness that tension, that spring
from which so much of life seems to release.
In the body, one multitude,
in the multitude, one body.

What Comes Next

With the curtain still drawn,
the gentleness of him
as he lay, dreaming and gorgeous,
his brow furrowed longingly
and eyelids shimmering.

With plans so tenuous,
did we back into choosing
no more mornings like this?
Flight is hard enough
with just one life to uphold.
But we watched storms together
from the balcony, and we
traced each other in the flesh
with all our insecurities.

And even as I felt the pangs
of my other powers growing,
this last he awoke
within the very earth of me.

So if what comes next
is our unraveling,
at least there was a whole.
At least we were together
when the gates came down,
and we beheld visions of ourselves
as we could be.

The Leap

You put away the things that made your room
to REM's jangly, melancholy hit
one by one: the unworn soccer jerseys, the silo of umbrellas
forgotten by students splashing through
midterm panic deluge,
the holey, screen-printed tees from X/XL s of yore.
Playing decks rifled through over internet stats,
painted and cast on all sorts of table all over town, get stacked
and groomed into rows in cherry-picked shipping boxes.
Dust motes recirculated
by air conditioning and upset clothing cairns
stir in their erratic, precarious paths in the 5pm spotlight.
Will you become a beloved mote of human dust
floating overseas to Shanghai?
In the presence of unraveling uncertainties
rising like smoke signals, or the mystic's signs,
how do we decide?
We get up and never know what we're getting into,
perpetual volunteers without a cause,
and perhaps the key, the key to everything,
is unconditional enthusiasm.

Widening of the Ways

Skip-a
   dee
     dee
        dee
           dee
              dee
birds twang on the morning in July
when already cicada song is twirling down
in whirling dervishes twirl east to west
ahead of sunrise.
Skip-a
   dee
     dee
        dee
           dee
              dee
and the van trunk is open, wheels waiting to close in
on a fresh road, where maybe there will be picnic tables
and waterfalls beside the winding way to the tarmac.

Last night was our last supper,
of egg drop noodle soup
sprinkled with crisp scallions,
that we sipped and slurped on the balcony,
in view of the rusted bridge to nowhere
and the traffic bustling across the River.
Skip-a
   dee
     dee
        dee
           dee
              dee
we are joining into the ordinariness of changing things,
a pair instead of one and one, and I am mostly
looking forward with good cheer as I close the hatch,
watching you pull out before I pedal away
to whence I came.

Watcher

A gargoyle upon your roof, I meld with the night,
planted on each side of the shingled pitch
to learn the street you know so well.

I conjure the trees felled years ago
whose canopy shielded this clandestine retreat
and fill them in with orioles and climbing ropes.

Invisible, the slick whirs of sparse traffic
on skidding wheels and on the heels of sirens
will storm through the park for deliverance.

This space where no one thinks to look,
in a world fixated on the slit at eye level —
you never told me that it was beautiful.

Hunched, still, the heat leaks upon my back
from the sagging, comfortable house, under its bower
of glittering telephone wires and motley purple clouds.

Skin grows scales in flecking beads of water
and lights snap out through the rows
like plinks of rain.

Marriage For All

Scraps of silk beseiged the capitol
on the day the decree was received.

Turnings of the other cheek for a kiss
blocked by the beaming of jubilant lips

were everywhere to be seen.
Bodies painted technicolor, over bruises

unforgotten from a dimmer past
soared along the greenway boulevard, and embraced.

A dream so long imagined, then and now
from state hall to state hall, paper to paper,

parade to hopeful, flamboyant parade.
And across the newsprint
heralding this history's end and wayward means,

splotches of pixelated, thunderous victory
softened by warm tears at the kitchen table.

Water Acro

The shifted sines of waves
made flat from atop slippery shoulders
mesmerize in a green screen
waiting to break my voluntary topple.
A lifeguard paddled out just for us
in the white rescue canoe,
for the two early merpeople of the lake
under a pearly, overcast sea.
We might as well give her a show —
a progression of quick failures,
wobbly nail-biters, rapid improvement,
and at last! A victorious climbing of a human
by a human, among the shifted sines of waves.

Picnic Blanket

Under the blanket, light filters through
in a painting of brilliant *ombré* dots
blending from spring green to turquoise tile.
Single threads are limned delicately, soft and bright.

In this tent of an autumn afternoon,
held up at times by a lone arm or leg,
your face is decomposed
into its beautiful curves, in golden white,
and I have felt no greater peace
than this, in simply beholding you,
the view interrupted
only by sparse waves of grass.

A Moment Bottled For You

There was just a firefly
on the other side of a screen door and I
got very close to it, and then
went out onto the deck and looked
at the many more stars visible here,
including the barest hint of milky way dust,
and I took in the dry lightning flashing,
and I thought of those tiny star photons
melding with my eyes. I wondered
whether I've ever been struck by light from a star
that made some of the atoms in my body.
And I thought of you and how amazing
love between two bodies is.

Vision of Another Self

If I were to draw an outline in the air
then throw it to the breeze,
could I send it to your mountain-limned corridor
among the lakes of China?

After many thousand leagues,
would it float up by your window,
open to errant fireworks displays?
Would you recognize it as by my hand
and catch it, with yours?

I stand on the shore of my own life,
and the catch between two people is so vast,
yet so close, within the slightest gasp of space.
We are such fluid and minute things.

So there seems nothing to do here, except perhaps
to dance, to draw the shape of what's to come,
to let it fly ahead of myself, my skyward guide,
and then to swim forth and deep.

Ergo, Ego, Go

This miraculous concert of cells
reaches, grasps, pulls, shakes,
calculates a move to make,
simulates and averts disaster,
knows which steps to take,
all effortless, as in sleep.

Am I the bumbling buffoon,
baton in hand, blunt and blundering,
banging chords asunder, as I
signal the double basses on the
wrong beat, gesturing blindly
for my body and brain
to obey the incompetent treatment of today?

Perhaps if I just dissolved offstage
and out of the way, then the orchestra
would play as it was meant to,
hummingly connected, alert, like a bouncing ray
in a glass bauble of light.

Daydream of You, Who Are Far Away

My Love is making spicy tea for me
  with juice exuding from the leaves.
My Love is kissing me while the kettle sings
  and February is panting at the window pane
  making steam.

Our love is laughing until tears
  and tears until laughter
and these moments we sink into, then remember
  of humid pockets carved into winter
  with the warmth of mingling breath
  and bliss become surrender.

Just Kids

Do you remember the cleft toward the base of the wall
we used to pinpoint among the fledgling trees?

Our feet wrapped around the angled granite bulges
before the slow but eager pull up and over the lip.

No small-city police ever patrolled those fields at night,
ratting out the sinners with iron-fist flashlights.

Throughout the alleyways in between
the sprinklers and the batting cages,
the chain link outfield fence and drifted soccer nets,

we meandered and spent the time
of the hazy, unsuspecting moon
dime by shiny dime, casting each into the pool-puddled grass;

it was the only rain that Providence had seen
in many many-flowered weeks.

Will we stop here? Will the frisbee disks of football beams
fringing your cheek
grow even more breath-catching in their flight?

The glowing cavern of May's underlit foliage closes
in like a veil around our shoulders,

until I am no longer dressed in devil's black,
nor you in angel's white.

Connection

Curtains form the train of the wind's cloak,
whose presence we only sense by what it moves.

The day feels like a man too long asleep
and woken up grown over with outdated truths.

Did I imagine that adventure would never snap open
like a sail convexly blown?

Did I imagine that it would end,
that we would then retire quietly
among lakes and glittering peach orchards?

In what other century
could our lives tangle so
and continue interleaving?

In what other time could I rise in the morning
and wish you a longing goodnight
half an earth away?

Embers

From brown hills to black I fly,
within a whirring darkness of solitude
until, like a sordid lava rope,
like a sore swollen to burst, the city lies poised
to ooze in overflow.
I am resting in the fire,
moving as a state of rest.
For sometimes it is harder to stay put;
sometimes it is easier to revel in restlessness.

And I am soaking in the kerosene,
I am soaking in the ire,
I am as meant to burn as a parched pine torch
sent by messenger in the night.
I am quickening in the thick of it,
I am sickening and yet not sick,
I am becoming like the trunk
whose bark curls away in flame.

And what is burning, anyway,
this thing within all things?
It feels as though a stream from peak to peak
recovering less than what's been spent.
It is not without its hazards
but it is not without its charms;
enchantments of its whiskey light
are still singing in my veins.
Set against life's duller poisons,
what price to pay?

Blowing on Coals

All the people apart in this world,
it makes me feel that
the fulfillment of the future
is in all loves meeting once again.
But probably
there are nobler acts
than the ones required for that end.
Maybe there is a future
more loving to be made
than that of isolated springs of love.

I like to think
that love could be a matrix
in which all people are suspended.
We would know its presence
from our movement through its current.

But then again, love is like a livewire
crackling between people, or a seed
to be tended, and to love everyone
seems impossible.
Still, perhaps when I see a bus driver
or a banker, I can smile
and mean it with much the same warmth
as with I attend to you.

Wealth

There is sparkle in the window screen
through which steam billows out
into lustrous autumn air.

The sun comes down like flaxen threads
ready to harvest and spin into songs
praising warmth and troves of simple goodness.

Radiating deep beneath the water,
cooled by the breeze on the surface,
my skin rippling with sensation.

And with each breath I am so glad
of the leaves starting to sound like rain
in all of their collisions, and I behold

the peeling paint of the windowsill,
but there's gorgeousness there, too —
in the contrast between grime and gleam,

in the starkness of the shadows underneath —
and I know that any homely thing is only so
for an impoverished eye and imagination.

Assurance

Sometimes living in the rhyme of the past
and the silence of the future,
I forget that the sky has split,
revealing white, and will always
be more beautiful than before.
I forget that there will be a time
when you will take the subway downtown,
take a ferry to a lobby
where people inch along like a caterpillar
with luggage wheels the tips
of ridiculous legs.
And that feeling the realness
of your body again
after a comma in our love
is one of the best parts of life.

Contact

I.
Dragging deep
and sweet in sinking
fight my way out
of words unspoken
taut my heartbeat
young unthinking
slow to realize
all the things I don't know.

Nightfall whispers
all the things you should know.

Letting go, sinking past
the point of no return,
I don't live
without mistakes —
running forsaken road.
Let's revolve around
all the things we should know.

II.
Like magnets made of liquid amber
pulling dragonfly to doom
or a disembodied light
coaxing midnight gypsy moths to flame,
so do gazes make me dance,
make me glance in darting strokes
to know whether my limbs draw in your eyes
beauty like blood.

Crows

It is easier to destroy,
so I destroy,
knowing
very well indeed
that what is created is
immensely more
precious.

They spear the ground
with gleaming, ruthless harpoons
and jerky movements, night comical
but for the shivery fierceness of their crowns.
They pirouette and sinuate
as the subterranean tectonic currents
that roil languid
and circulate transformation
shimmering in flecks of sunlight.

They are not concerned,
see and roost (Do they dream?)
uninhibited by morality
by the chitinous deaths
that have tumbled down their throats
into satisfaction.

Will you undo me? he says.
I love you, I love you, but I am sick,
I say.
My love is stronger, I will wait.

How could I wound you, knowing as I do?
I remove my fingers from my mouth,
my fingers from the mangled grass.
You will, and I will still love you,
beyond warrant, beyond pain.

They stare at me without fear, without judgment,
those raucous wraiths,
and drift, until their reflection upon the waves,
and the waves, are almost same.

Caution to the Winds

The danger we try to have
but try to leave.
Unsure of whether
we kindle disaster,
what words for feelings
too encompassing to speak.
The difficulty is discerning
when to quit —
when to cleave through
the growing tree.
The tree's amputation—stump—
remaining in my heart,
whose passions, at least
did not consume me.

Part III

Rolling Away the Stone

An unacknowledged hurt, which amplifies
memory of its source, until my outward eyes
are saturated not with what is real,
but a flash of myth, a distortion,
arising from a blight refused to heal.

And the spirit that rejoices,
the spirit that combines
laughter, hope, lightheartedness,
I feel as though has died.
A child with useless limb within me cries.

My being is weighed down to the quick of it,
has been sickening, and now is sick
from two dreams tainted through with grief:
the one whose loss I did not choose,
the other which I chose to keep,
which even in its sweetness does not bring relief.

So the time has come for reckoning
with this deadness, still surreal,
that claims a fragment of my being
and makes all forgetting brief.
I am somewhere wasteland, apart and unrevealed
and in consuming question mark abide.

One Breath of Flame

You, whose paths not understood
writhe in closed recesses of the mind,
lie sleepless while lamp beams swing across the wall —
dream, while half your body yearns for flight,
of a dream when dreams shall no more uproot you.

Can't you see me, o double mine?
A wild spark transfigured into night,
an opus near unwritten out of strife,
a song near severed with a knife.
And what for do you ruin me, most euphoric of delights,
if our blistered soul is shared?

I cannot teach you like a child,
excise you like a growth,
refute you like a philosopher's logician.
We are not like two sides of a single coin,
but like two trunks diverging from one spine.
We balance, rise together
and in our images combine;
the world, and the world within can never tell
which mark is yours, and which is mine.

Poison From the Wound

Corroding the fiber of my veins
like the drops of drugs I did not take,
but were infused while I was not awake,
my own blood betrays the thirst it slakes.

This is the pursuer one cannot outrun
and a vise that one cannot escape,
but a foe that one can also not embrace
without surrender to a wretched state.

I rise and reckon with what will has done
after four seasons lived out in disarray —
of feelings I could neither let go, dissolve, outpace,
nor store within a safer place.

Forest Fire

Heart rapid misfires,
abdomen pulsating with burn,
every five minutes, the emotional pop-up
recurs, which will not let me forget the past.

Behind every disastrous failure,
there is a thin membrane of joy
poised to rebound,
though I cannot tell its time.
When I am in the grip of something,
even when it is myself
that must do the releasing,
I never know
how much breath I have left,
or when the fresh gasp will come.

And when I am seized,
it is as though into a world
with no sight and no sound;
there are moments when
all that cuts through
is an awareness of the will to endure,
even if I do not come out the same —
though I could not even say
who I was or where I am going.

I am waiting for a new breath
as I feel the old layers die —
as I force the old feelings to burn.

Page Not Found

I am looking for a poem
in my blue and faithful paperback
that will tell me what I want to know.
Surely it must lie in the section titled,
'Resurrection', or perhaps, 'Work',
or even, 'O Lord'.
All of these people
tuning carefully into life —
someone has to have found
the meaning and the words
to give the meaning breath.
But I cannot find the poem.
I am sitting with a magnetic pulse
seizing up the basin of my mind
until my skull encloses a white-hot ache —
and I just want someone to tell me
that I am now just
a whole with more pieces
and not a thing broken apart.

Siphon

With this page I am bottling up my sadness,
instead of bottling it up,
and words are the siphon of toxins from a wound.
Nothing is to be taken so seriously
that you cannot speak of it.

If you are counting in the dark
the reasons why words should remain
but pangs felt in the body,
know that the bridge between thinking and moving,
sometimes we call it darkness,
sometimes we call it light.

When I am done with this page,
I can hold it up to the morning beams
flooding through the pantry window,
among the other glinting jars.

I can feel the liquid's warmth through the glass,
and respect its power without being dissolved.
And the white peeling door swollen with summer
will squeak closed behind me.

The Verdant Doorway

To the right there is a doorway to the garden
where you are waiting for me,
and sunset rains down between the leaves.

And whenever I feel the call of deadening paths
I lift my face to the promise of its breeze.

In that garden the soil holds all the promises
that we cannot grow where we are.

They are the fruits for which we have to leave
if we are ever to know the places
where they live to touch the light.

Following the Trail

The greater the resolve with which
I examine the origins of mistakes,
the subtler they become.
Sometimes one begins
as a slight puff of wind twisted awry
visible only by the dust it carries.
It has so little substance of its own,
and yet,
in pattern and varied repetition
becomes strong;
with a center of emptiness
it peels away the shingles of the roof
that keeps the rain out.

So often when I slip it is just a thought
that could have simply disappeared
but instead remained, and that I did not
into harmonious current give new shape,
for I had not the awareness
nor the imagination to foresee
the deafening crush of a tornado
within the whisper of a breeze.

One Promise

One
promise
I will
keep:

to love
each
breath

to love
each
success

to love
each
mistake

to cherish
each
laugh

to hold
each
piece

to love
each
day

to love
in the
dark

Honing

To find out what is essential
is a process of destruction —
of tearing down,
of searing away the bark,
of throwing water on the fireworks
cavorting in our hearts.
I am never certain that when I am done,
there will be any heart left.

As though a great bell had thrummed
almost too low to hear,
one morning I woke up with a wound
which was somehow seeping light.
I knew that as it closed
I would have to open. I would have to
love through love, to the other
side of love, leaving behind
what I thought *was* love.
The heart is not just what we feel,
but what we believe.
To tear it down is an act of belief
in what could be.

A Tower of the Mind

High up in the tower
are my carpets made of stone;
another sunset settles over
ramparts in violent tones,

and to my right are doorways
into tunnels of unease,
leading outward from the chamber
where I behold them from my knees.

The lion paces in the thunder
in her trance of solitude,
so majestic that I wonder
if she is my tribute to Saint Jude.

All of heaven is my ceiling,
all of heaven is my roof,
and she is shaming all the starlight,
my body paralyzed, removed.

If I could rise then I would hasten,
renounce these doorways made of haze
thin as whispers in the space
called dominion by the saints.

And the lion, she would claim
her rightful stance among the spheres,
and this tower, now my prison,
would be the place where I had risen.

Traded Time

What appeared the seat of sickness
was in fact the buried seed
of betterment destined for becoming,
and not the dominion of disease.
Examining the underside
of a resting fallen tree,
what rot I envisioned was the bursting
of fresher roots within me.

Sinking into quicksand
with the flailing of replay,
swallowed by the tapes unwound,
rewound, resounding waves
perpetuated by a button-press,
as though were to engrave
the past in perfect instants
upon the foil of the brain.

So was memory — so unseeing
the desire to continue what is gone
that remained
when the present held
nothing but itself, that I gave
a song for a broken record
and demanded that it play.

To Hatred Transmute:

First, to fully believe
that we can choose the way we feel;
that we can gradually lay again
the foundations of the mind
to make ready a space for the unexpected,
the uncomfortable, and those things
which simply cannot be simplified.

Bothered

These days, there is a broken doorknob
that I know I cannot fix;
it does not lie within my property.
But I walk past it
all the time,
because it does lie
within my neighborhood.
The owner has to know about it;
it must affect them every day.
Either they square off, hands in pockets,
with the little devil head on,
or they clamber in through a window,
roughing up their designer suit
and carefully prepared exterior.
Each time, the fight on both sides
is exactly the same:
the fight to do nothing,
the fight to disengage.

And this is how I learned
that I, too, have a broken doorknob
to the back porch of my heart.

The Tiger and the Turtle

In ambition a tiger, in love a turtle
the one,
in love a tiger, in ambition a turtle
the other.

One over-greets, the other retreats,
for which reason the tiger
once more affection seeks —
until the toothy turtle, brooding in its shell
on occasions over days and into weeks,
snaps — at the smothering it perceives.
But the tiger only wants to know
that the turtle is not about to leave;
with Beloved solidly at its side,
there's no cause to fear
that its heart will be denied.
But the turtle wants to venture out
within a sacred space;
anxiety ensues when it suspects
independence might be—erased.
It does not love the tiger less,
but itself desires to preserve.

I am the turtle in retreat
with a tiger at the gate —
fighting to undo my armor,
expose my heart, and speak.

Flitting, Steadfast

Is it fair, my dear, to induct on love?
This moment, this trés blissful exchange,
does it really ensure forever's reign?

Tomorrow and tomorrow and tomorrow
are not lined up like dominoes
to be flicked with one finger, all downed in a string
or skewered with one arrow through the middling.
In the gilded lapse, where dispersion's supreme,
connection will never be guaranteed.

So think not of a line that we traverse
but of a space where we spread out,
root downward, immerse.
And maybe many times in all our meanderings
we will touch hands, and be at peace.

Ripe

It is a more complicated happiness,
this smile with a teardrop
suspended in its source;
or a rising over wreckage
time has not yet buried or dissolved.
The question is, do I regret?
Would I, in forgetting,
reclaim that weightless joy
unenriched by dark's contrast?
The ingot by which I nearly drowned
is becoming an anchor in the sound.

Rhyme

I surprised you with a picnic, in the park,
a year after, when,
underneath the paper lanterns,
we met up —
on the grass carpet of a dance floor
where my heart within me shivered
and shook out golden drops.

And the ocean bay before us
was just a multitude of drops,
which in their particularities merged
into the cusp of the sublime.
The sounds of time never repeat
but may, in special seasons, rhyme.

Favorite

Your socks are on the table again,
the string beans of socks, emerald and elegant,
long enough to envelope your calf, like a round seed.
Three years ago, in the concept of my home,
such a configuration would have been impossible —
would not have computed —
a sock does not permit itself to idle upon a table,
no more than a table permits a sock to idle upon its face.
I sit, confronting the impossible,
navigating the fretful smog exuded from my abdomen
and polluting my bloodstream.
Do I move them?
I could put them in the refrigerator,
with the other string beans;
I could fold them into the utensil drawer
for theater of the absurd.
I could instead attempt to reason with you
on the proper order of the universe.
But then the curious imp in me,
sees the curious imp in you,
the clever monkey without civilization
but with ample sense.
It is a miracle, after all, that it has survived
every curbing influence from the cradle
to now lay the socks upon the table.
I do not have the heart to quash it,
your monkeyish spark.

Is this a hymn to chaos?
Is this a hymn to love?
Is it love that, despising everyone's chaos but our own,
makes one exception?
Or perhaps no exception at all — that being too much,
reorders the entire world
just so that within it, our favorite monkey can fit.

The Hard Way

I sing in praise of grit, without which
nary a worthy thing would be done, or overcome
or the better part of life obtained.
I sing of bitter sweats and what begets
the bracing rebirth of the mind.
Comfort was never the condensing cloud
from which the elements of thriving burst,
nor the feel of standing at the envisioned crest
and beholding time's revelatory hand.

Determined

Among all the ways you are and that I love,
today's is the way you eat your mango.
Peeling back the light skin in petals,
you cradle the oval flesh like a little sun.

You press the tanginess against your lips,
taking care not one drop of juice escapes;
you savor the first bite, then wait
for the moment of perfect readiness for the next.

You do not eat half-heartedly
or absent-mindedly. You are intent upon bliss.
And without fumbles or distraction you go after it,
applying the gentle force of the morning and a paring knife.

Cumulus

Every once in a while,
the rusting legions of the soul
need a good war.
Too much peace can degrade
into its own kind of dysfunction.
The struggle between
explosive change and consistency
is always being waged
in some corner of
the mind-cloud of heaven.

Exchange

In a pore upon this scab of earth
risen from the fires through the ocean.
You know I am not free.
You know how I am strong despite.

The hopping streets in spring again
etched in the pavement tablet of the city.
I move among them as I will.
You know I am not free.
I am closer.
I am at the edge.
I can dash my fingers through
the incubus smoke of you.
Be free, you say.
Go wherever it is you will.

But I do not want freedom.
I want love.
I want emancipation not of my life,
but of my being.
I know you cannot make me free.
And so I remember you as you were
when you so softly dreamed.

Crutches

In the beginning,
we latch onto the tiny, tiny things
we think we know about each other
to construct, from a galaxy,
a single photograph
or movie reel.
And oh, are they enchanting.

You know you are getting somewhere
when you can let them go,
when you can accept in your core
that they say more about you
than the other.
You know you are getting somewhere
when your feelings are not about
how the other will make blossom
your dreams of self-expansion.
When the other is not the reason for existence
or the instrument of your betterment;
but are, as they are, the reason for love.

Kingdom Come

The visitation of a humble angel, a grace,
you are hanging the laundry
patiently, piece by piece.
We are all half-breaking
in the predictable and ordinary ways.
I know it is the heart of me
which makes you divine.
But that we are mortal,
that our bodies use
until they are used up
is the nebula of the divine
within us.

I do not want one big day, after which
flowers will be discarded,
impressions of the food exchanged,
normalcy assumed.
I want one million blossoms
of the feeling of holding you,
and the knowledge
that we gathered what could be ours
when there was still
time.

Epilogue

Loving what's good for you.
A happiness complicated
by the condition that when we want
we are not letting go of wanting.
A part of us has broken off,
unable to appreciate blessings.
Over and over I ask
why it is broken.
But that does not help it
resume a new place.

I must confess that I do not speak to you
knowing how this goes.
Reconciliation of the splices
within our living soul
might only be the extension of that same touch
upon the living soul between us all.

Learning to love peace
even after craving it.
Learning to love arrival
even when we are arrived.
Learning to dwell in completion
even when we are complete.
Even when our living soul is healed
and ready for release.

Gratitude does not have enough words in the English language to capture its depths and subtleties. I am so grateful to the Clare Songbirds Publishing House team for seeing something of value in my work and for carrying this collection through to publication. I hope to deliver on the confidence that inspired them to give me my first major break.

I am grateful to all the Toronto poets who have welcomed me into their midst, encouraged me, and provided opportunities to share my work. It is the direct person-to-person sharing of poetry that is most purposeful to me. Thank you for listening to my words and for guiding me to other amazing individuals.

I am grateful to the people who enabled me to write the pieces in this collection by way of our interactions. I believe that I have gained — dare I say it — wisdom from my experiences with you. This greater awareness of what is truly worth devoting my life to is the most precious gift that you could have given me.

Thank you.

Julia Gibson is a multidisciplinary thinker, creator, and problem solver who aspires to connect people, perspectives, and ideas toward a more understanding and compassionate world. After studies in violin performance at Manhattan School of Music, she earned a BA in Cognitive Science from Brown University and an MSc in Mathematics from McMaster University. She currently works in aerospace engineering and is active in the Toronto poetry scene. Her poetry explores topics such as socio-economic inequality, LGBTQ+ issues, cross-country cycling, the natural world, and womanhood in the twenty-first century. When neither tinkering nor writing, she can usually be found in the studio learning Afro-Caribbean dances. Her personal website is at www.julia-gibson.com. You can also follow her on Instagram @julia.f.gibson.

www.ingramcontent.com/pod-product-compliance
Lightning Source LLC
Chambersburg PA
CBHW062039120526
44592CB00035B/1680